ISRAELI MOSAICS

ISRAELI MOSAICS

of the Byzantine Period

INTRODUCTION BY

ERNST KITZINGER

A MENTOR-UNESCO ART BOOK

PUBLISHED BY
THE NEW AMERICAN LIBRARY, INC.
BY ARRANGEMENT WITH UNESCO

FIRST PRINTING, DECEMBER, 1965

MENTOR TRADEMARK REG. U. S. PAT. OFF. AND FOREIGN COUNTRIES
REGISTERED TRADEMARK—MARCA REGISTRADA

MENTOR-UNESCO ART BOOKS ARE PUBLISHED BY
THE NEW AMERICAN LIBRARY, INC.
1301 AVENUE OF THE AMERICAS, NEW YORK, NEW YORK 10019

PRINTED IN ITALY BY AMILCARE PIZZI S.P.A., MILANO

The mosaics illustrated in this book have as an historical setting the flowering of the Holy Land in the period of Byzantine rule. From the time of the destruction of the Jewish Temple in the year 70 after Christ until the early fourth century the Roman province of Palaestina, of which modern Israel comprises a large part, existed in relative obscurity. Though there had been a temporary upswing under the Antonine and Severan emperors, a large-scale economic and cultural revival of the country began with the official recognition of Christianity under Constantine the Great (306-37). The imperial government, established in its new capital on the Bosphorus, sponsored the erection of sumptuous buildings on the major sites associated with the life of Christ. The Holy Places soon began to attract pilgrims from far and wide. The fifth and sixth centuries—the period to which nearly all the mosaics here reproduced belong—were a time of peace and prosperity. The Persian invasion of the early seventh century and the subsequent conquest of the country by the Arabs put an end to this era. The mosaicists' art, however, still flourished under the early Ummaiyyad caliphs, who, vying with their Byzantine opponents, adopted the medium for their own buildings.

The adornment of floors with richly patterned mosaics—and all ancient mosaics which have survived in Israel are pavements—was part of the common artistic heritage of the Graeco-Roman world. The soil of every country that was once part of the Roman Empire has yielded examples. No other pictorial medium offers a material so evenly and widely distributed in time and space to the student of the history of art in the Roman and early Byzantine period;

none permits such close and detailed observation of major trends during this vital era of transition, which saw the breakdown and disintegration of classical art and the emergence of those new concepts, themes, and styles that were to mature eventually in the art of the Latin, Byzantine and Islamic Middle Ages. Within this broad category of monuments the floor mosaics of Israel (and those of the adjacent areas of Jordan, Syria, and Lebanon) have a particular significance, partly because of their relatively advanced date and the witness they thus bear to the final stages of the process of transition just referred to, and partly because of certain special circumstances peculiar to the region.

In Roman times floor mosaics had been associated chiefly with secular architecture, both private and public, and only to a lesser extent with religious buildings. The secular uses of the medium continued in the Byzantine and early Islamic eras—for instance, of the Palestinian mosaics illustrated here, that on Plates 4 and 5 adorned a villa; that on Plates 19 to 21 a bath; that on Plate 28 an Ummaiyyad palace—but, in general, there was after the fourth century a far greater incidence of ornate pavements in religious contexts. Christians, at least in some parts of the Empire, had begun to adorn the floors of their churches with mosaics as early as the Constantinian period. The Jews followed suit very soon. Synagogues with mosaic floors have been unearthed in recent decades in various parts of the ancient world, but nowhere in greater numbers, or with a richer and more interesting repertory of pictorial representations, than in Israel.

Pictorial decoration of the floor in rooms destined for religious purposes poses special problems. There are obvious limitations to the representation of sacred subjects in places which are liable to be trodden on. An imperial decree of the year 427 prohibiting the representation of crosses on floors is an indication of sensitivity on this score in the period which concerns us here. Thus the mosaicist designing a pavement for a church or a synagogue (or the patron who commissions such work) moves in much narrower limits than the designer of wall or vault decorations for these buildings. He will be tempted to a much greater extent to stay within the traditional secular repertory inherited from Roman times. The restriction imposed on the use of specifically religious imagery adds to the natural tendency of the craftsman—and most pavement mosaics are the work of artisans rather than artists—to perpetuate time-honoured patterns and motifs. Blatantly pagan themes, of course, will generally be avoided. But there was a vast reservoir of neutral and innocuous imagery, especially from the world of nature and country life, ready to be drawn on freely; hence the large number of mosaics on the floors of churches and synagogues depicting animals and plants, hunts, rural scenes, and the like. The designer of the two beautiful panels in the transept wings of the church at Tabgha (Plates 1 and 2)— the church which enshrines the reputed site of Christ's miraculous feeding of the multitudes—made use of a favourite theme of late Hellenistic and Roman floor decoration, namely, the scenery of the swamp lands of the Nile with their characteristic flora, wildlife, and architecture (which includes even a Nilometer). The trees, the leaping leopard, and the other wild animals which adorn the border of a floor in a church at Caesarea (Plate 26) are elements from the subject category "rural landscape with hunters", a theme particularly familiar from the floor mosaics in the houses of wealthy Roman landowners in North Africa, but known to decorators of private houses also in Palestine itself, witness the border of a pavement in a villa at Beth-Guvrin (Plates 4 and 5). The hen with its chicks depicted on the floor of the synagogue at Beth-Alpha (Plate 14) and the hen laying an egg which forms part of a rich and splendid mosaic in a synagogue at Ma'on (Plate 24) are other motifs from the rural repertory, much of which must have been codified in pattern books. Otherwise the rather stereotyped occurrence of the same motifs in mosaics widely separated in time and space, and the appearance of a number of animals and other motifs of which the mosaicists could hardly have had first-hand knowledge, would be difficult to explain.

Tradition therefore lies heavily on this art, more heavily still than it does on other artistic media which Christians and Jews took over from their Graeco-Roman environment. The pavements of churches and synagogues have a special interest precisely on this account. They offer a singularly intriguing spectacle of pagan survivals. At the same time, the narrow limits imposed on changes and innovations lend poignancy to the artist's success in nevertheless conveying new messages and expressing the spirit and aspirations of a new age.

Christians and Jews did not go entirely parallel ways in taking over the medium and adapting it to their needs. Examples of the first phase of Christian floor decoration, prominently represented in the West by the sumptuous early fourth-century mosaics at Aquileia, have not been encountered so far in Palestine or anywhere else in the East. The hallmark of these earliest Christian floors is an exuberant display of animal, marine, pastoral, and other genre subjects, with a relatively small number of distinctively Christian scenes and symbols providing definite religious accents. There followed in the late fourth century a puritanical phase in which figure representations were banished from church pavements almost entirely. This was the heyday of geometric all-over designs (a type of decoration which was to enjoy a special vogue again later under the Arab caliphs: see Plate 28). Floors composed entirely of geometric and other conventional patterns continued in frequent use also in fifth- and sixth-century churches (Plate 7). Sometimes a cross will be included in the design, and it is quite clear that the law of the year 427 did not, in fact, put an end to this practice (Plate 6). But what is most characteristic of the decoration of church floors after the year 400 is the breaking-down of puritanical austerity, and now it is the Eastern Mediterranean world—Palestine included—which leads the movement. Very occasionally an Old Testament scene will appear on a floor; for instance, the pavement in the nave of a church at Beth-Guvrin displays in one of its compartments the story of Jonah. But chiefly it is the neutral animal and plant genre which gradually infiltrates (or re-infiltrates?) the church pavement. The relevance of this imagery to a Christian context is in many instances far from evident. Artists and patrons

8

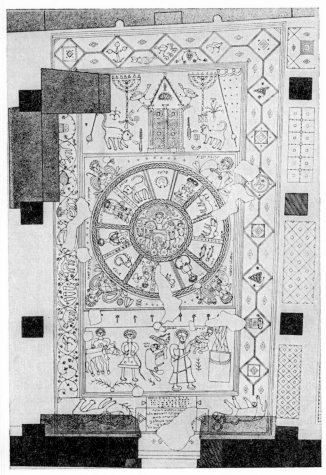

Beth-Alpha, synagogue. General view of pavement (see details, Plates 8 to 14). Sixth century. Photo: The Hebrew University of Jerusalem.

9

themselves may not always have had a very clear idea in this respect. One suspects that their choice of subjects was determined to a considerable extent by the fact that the repertory was part of the mosaicist's workshop tradition. Whatever religious motivation was proffered to justify its being displayed on the church floor may often have been *ex post facto*, variable, and lacking in precision. For the modern observer this opens up a wide field of speculation. Presumably the nature genre was meant to stand for such broad themes as God's Creation and the Earthly Paradise. But in many instances it is impossible to say what prompted or excused the choice of a specific subject in a particular context. The display of Nilotic motifs in the Church the Multiplication of the Loaves and Fishes is a case in point (Plates 1 and 2).

The pictorial elaboration of church floors reaches a climax in the sixth century. The variety of motifs is now greater than ever, with nature subjects still predominating. At the same time the meaning of this repertory within the context of the church building tends to become less vague, thanks to explanatory inscriptions and other factors. On the one hand, a figure or group may be endowed with a straightforward religious content. For instance, an animal scene may be accompanied by a biblical text such as a quotation from the Prophet Isaiah's Vision of the Peaceable Kingdom ("the lion shall eat straw like the ox") and thus acquire an explicit and highly pertinent message. On the other hand, nature subjects may be provided simply with identifying labels indicating that these subjects were considered a legitimate part of church decoration in their own right. A landscape picture may bear the names of specific towns or countries; a series of rustic human figures, those of the twelve months of the year which they are meant to personify (Plates 15 and 16). Pictorial "catalogues" of this kind are frequent at this time. This encyclopaedic element foreshadows the sculptured decoration of mediaeval cathedrals with their systematic representation of nature subjects. No doubt, as in the case of the latter, there was an intention to proclaim the physical world as an integral part of the Christian universe.

Thus the seemingly irrelevant repertory of the floor decorator was at last harnessed firmly to the meaning and purpose of the church building. The tendency to make the imagery of the church pavement more distinctly meaningful in terms of an over-all programme also leads, in some instances, to a differentiation in the choice of subjects for the nave and the sanctuary respectively. It is in the nave—often identified in Christian symbolic thinking with the created world—that the themes pertaining to the physical universe are most frequently located, while the more palpably religious themes (which are apt to relate to texts cited in the liturgy) are often placed in, or near, the sanctuary, the part of the church which symbolizes the spiritual and celestial world. One of the most remarkable instances of a floor mosaic with a direct and unmistakable religious meaning occurs at Tabgha, where in the sixth century a panel with two fishes flanking a basket of bread was placed behind the altar in direct proximity to the stone on which Christ was said to have performed the miracle of the loaves and fishes (Plate 3). Many of the holy sites in Palestine at one time were adorned with images which called up before the pilgrim's eye the biblical events associated with them. The Tabgha mosaic—so eloquent in its terseness and simplicity—is the only such representation to have survived.

Archaeological finds in Israel provide singularly rich opportunities to compare with the development of floor decoration in churches the concurrent development in synagogues. Today, especially since the discovery of the third-century synagogue at Dura-Europos with its extensive cycles of biblical wall-paintings, the occurrence of pictorial representations in Jewish houses of worship of the late antique and early Byzantine periods is no longer a source of surprise. The Second Commandment had ceased to be interpreted literally by large sections of Jewry long before the first animate figures appear on Jewish pavements. Floor decoration of synagogues sprang from, and was sustained by, the same Graeco-Roman workshop tradition which was the source of its Christian counterpart. Specifically Jewish elements were introduced, as we shall see

11

Beth-Shean, monastery of the Lady Mary. General view of pavement with the personifications of the Months (see details, Plates 15 and 16). Probably 569 after Christ. Photo: The University Museum, University of Philadelphia.

presently, but they were embedded in a neutral genre taken again from the world of nature and rural life and posing the same difficult—or, indeed, insoluble—problems of interpretation which we have encountered in considering church floors (Plates 11 to 14, 23, 24). It is safe to assume that in many cases the same ateliers worked for both Christian and Jewish patrons. For instance, the pavement of the synagogue at Ma'on is so similar to that of a church at nearby Shellal (which bears an inscription of 561/62) that both must be attributed to the same workshop. The famous floor of the synagogue at Beth-Alpha with its touchingly naïve pictures, executed, as the inscription says, by Marianos and his son Hanina, is a case of two folk artists (evidently Jewish, judging by the latter name) being employed by a local community, perhaps in a proud demonstration of self-sufficiency. But even this untutored team, which also worked in a synagogue building at nearby Beth-Shean, used much of the traditional repertory.

An essential difference between the Christian and the Jewish development (so at least it would appear on the strength of the finds known at present) is that the latter was ahead of the former so far as the introduction of articulate and specific subject matter was concerned. To represent nature themes encyclopaedically and with identifying labels was, as we have seen, an innovation in the decoration of church floors in the sixth century. At least one representation of this kind made its appearance in Jewish floor mosaics at a substantially earlier date: namely, the portrayal of the twelve signs of the zodiac, each with its name inscribed, in a radial arrangement with the Chariot of the Sun in the centre and with personifications of the Four Seasons surrounding it (Plates 11 and 12). No representation of this subject has so far come to light in a church. On floors of Palestinian synagogues, however, there are at least four examples, and one of these—a floor discovered at Hammath (Tiberias) in 1961—is thought to be of the fourth century. Originally (and more appropriately) a subject for ceilings, the zodiac had migrated on to the pavement in the Roman period when many ceiling and floor designs began to be used interchangeably.

13

What specific meaning, or meanings, it assumed in the context of the synagogue floor must for the present remain uncertain. But it unquestionably introduced into that context an explicitly cosmological theme.

Synagogue floors also began to display at the same relatively early date an unequivocally religious element. This, too, takes a form unknown (or, at any rate, never so fully elaborated) on church floors: that of an array of ritual utensils. The objects normally represented include the *menorah* (or seven-branched candelabrum), the *torah* shrine, the *lulab* and *ethrog* (palm branch and citron), the *shofar* (or ram's horn) and the incense shovel (Plates 22 and 25). These liturgical objects are usually and appropriately placed in the furthest part of the nave, in the area adjacent to the *Aron ha-Kodesh*, the actual *torah* shrine. Set off, as they frequently are, against the zodiac or other nature subjects in the main part of the nave, they introduce into the imagery of the floor a meaningful polarity such as was evolved in the decoration of church floors only in the course of the sixth century.

The pictorial programme of the synagogue pavement appears in its most fully developed stage in the rustic work at Beth-Alpha. The zodiacal circle enclosing the Chariot of the Sun here occupies a dominant position in the centre of the nave (perhaps it was still consciously thought of as a reflexion of a domed ceiling). The panel of liturgical utensils—richly elaborated with two lions, two candelabra, and two sets each of *lulab*, *ethrog*, and incense shovel flanking the *torah* shrine, and with curtains framing the entire scene to emphasize its sacred character—adjoins the celestial image on the south side where the *Aron ha-Kodesh* was located. Balancing this panel on the north or entrance side is a third explicitly meaningful element, a biblical scene such as was included occasionally in the floor decoration both of synagogues and of churches. The subject represented, and developed in considerable detail, is the Sacrifice of Isaac, a scene of crucial and central significance in Jewish thought of the period, because of its implication of absolute obedience and submission to God's will and of God's solicitude for the truly faithful. The neutral nature and animal genre with its much vaguer symbolical implications is relegated to the framing bands surrounding the three panels.

The Beth-Alpha floor, according to the inscription at the entrance, was made in the time of Emperor Justin. The ruler referred to could be either Justin I (518-27) or Justin II (565-78) and it is difficult to decide between these alternatives. The period of the second Justin may be more likely, particularly in view of the fact that some of the motifs on the border of the pavement recall those of (non-Jewish) mosaics of the second half of the sixth century at nearby Beth-Shean. In any case, however, the two folk artists who executed the pavement can hardly have been innovators. If in their naïve handiwork the system and programme of Jewish floor decoration appears in its richest and most harmoniously balanced form, this can only mean that the system had reached its mature stage before their time.

Jewish pavement iconography thus appears to have developed faster than its Christian counterpart. Its heyday may well have been in the fifth and the first half of the sixth century. On the other hand, the pictorial decoration of synagogue pavements seems to have come to an end before that of church pavements. The floor at Ma'on shows that in the sixties of the sixth century good and elaborate work was still done in synagogues. But soon thereafter the Jewish development must have stopped altogether. While the pavements of Palestinian churches continued to be embellished with rich imagery as late as the year 600 (and later still) the Jews by this time seem to have reverted to a strict interpretation of the Second Commandment.

The history of pavement decoration in churches and synagogues—marked as it is both by parallelisms and by divergencies—thus throws interesting sidelights on the thoughts and attitudes of Christian and Jewish communities in Palestine in the early Byzantine period. It is the use of pictorial subjects and the choice and arrangement of these subjects which prove particularly revealing in this respect. But the floor mosaics of Israel are of interest also as documents in the history of style. The centuries to which they belong witnessed a major step in the aesthetic revolution of the post-classical period, a revolution comparable in its scope and magnitude to that which has taken place in the art of our own time. Artisans' products though they are, the mosaics clearly reflect that step.

A comparison of a leaping animal from the fifth-century floor of the villa at Beth-Guvrin (Plate 5) with a similar motif from a church floor at Caesarea which is more than a century younger (Plate 26) is instructive. At first sight the difference may not seem excessively great. Indeed there is evidently a continuity of techniques and workshop traditions linking the two representations. Yet the change is fundamental. The earlier artist fashions his animal as a figure in the round; the later one appears to think of it primarily as a pattern. Not only does he represent the leopard's spotted skin in a conventionalized manner, but the body itself also forms a pattern, with a brown stripe in the centre and an almost symmetrical arrangement of white, bluish and brown zones above and below. While superficially the artist may still convey an impression of highlights and shades, essentially his distribution of colours is ornamental. In the earlier mosaic, with its more sparing use of light tesserae and its more subtle distribution of dark tones, the body is modelled much more convincingly. To be sure, even the fifth-century mosaic is no longer a truly classical work. The heavy dark contour which surrounds nearly the entire figure of the animal is indicative of the degree to which, even then, conceptual methods of rendering reality had won out over methods based on actual observation. But the little hare of Beth-Guvrin is still a live body, and we readily yield to the artist's suggestion that the animal has taken a leap in " real " space. We see it in a stretch of open country with ground below its feet and trees in the background. The white ground of the Caesarea leopard, on the other hand, is nothing but a neutral foil.

Comparisons such as this can easily be multiplied. We may, for instance, consider side-by-side the birds from the fifth-century mosaics at Tabgha (Plates 1 and 2) and those

Nirim, synagogue of Ma'on. General view of pavement (see details, Plates 22 to 24). Sixth century. Photo: Israel Department of Antiquities and Museums.

of the sixth century from the bath at Tiberias (Plates 19 to 21). Again we observe in the later work an essentially ornamental use of colours which does little or nothing to suggest three-dimensional shapes. The patterned rendering extends even to the eyes, which resemble ornamental rosettes and give the effect of a lifeless stare, very different from the vivid—almost sly—glance which the Tabgha artist was able to impart to his birds by means of a judicious juxtaposition of tiny, irregularly shaped chips of black, white and red. It is characteristic of the style of the Tiberias mosaic that the birds should fit so neatly into the framework of interlacing bands by which they are surrounded (see especially Plate 20). Animate creature and inanimate pattern have, in fact, become a single, inseparable unit. Any suggestion of "real" space would be merely disturbing. The three-dimensional body has become as one with the surface, the background a firm and solid matrix for the design. By contrast, the neutral ground surrounding the birds at Tabgha might still be understood as "air" though even here the artist in distributing the elements of landscape setting has avoided all implications of depth.

This is a point which will be elaborated below, but for the moment let us consider merely the contrast which we have found in our comparisons of single figures, the antithesis between three-dimensional and two-dimensional renderings, between lifelike modelling and abstract pattern. This contrast is basic to the stylistic development not only of our mosaics, but of all pictorial art in the late antique and early Byzantine period. The development had begun long before the first of these Palestinian mosaics were made and was barely completed at the time to which the last of them belong. It was by no means a uniformly straightforward progress towards ever greater abstraction. The pace differed in different regions and indeed in different workshops; there were reactions and retrogressions, as well as sudden leaps forward; and there were all manner of different nuances due to diverse local traditions, individual preferences, and the meeting and merging of various influences. Of this entire complex picture the mosaics here illustrated give us only a limited view. But it is a characteristic view, not only in its clear indication of the over-all trend, but also in illustrating some of the diversities of the development.

The figures from the floors of the monastery at Beth-Shean (Plates 15 to 18) exemplify one stylistic variant. Attributable probably to the year 569, they are not as abstract as their relatively advanced date might lead one to expect. It is true that the artist no longer gives us a really convincing view of an organic body surrounded by space. His flautist (Plate 17), supposedly depicted in a three-quarter view as he sits on a wicker stool and plays to his dog, is actually shown with both his shoulders equidistant from the beholder (and thus merging into the surface pattern) and his seat in only superficial and precarious contact with the piece of furniture supporting him. These are tell-tale signs that the artist has lost interest in rendering objects accurately and in their true physical relationship (by comparison, how much more convincingly had the mosaicist at Beth-Guvrin a century or so earlier rendered the posture of his mounted huntsman: see Plate 4). Similarly, the turn of the dog's head, as depicted by the artist at Beth-Shean, defies the laws of anatomy. But, superficially at least, there is great liveliness in these figures, and this is due mainly to a rather bold and free use of colour accents in which all regularity is avoided. The artist is particularly successful in imparting lively and natural glances to the faces (see especially Plate 18). There is more of mediaeval solemnity and spirituality in the faces of the relatively large figures personifying the Months (Plates 15 and 16), but even in these colour accents are still applied with an almost impressionistic verve and boldness. The particular work-shop which was active here still had command of much of the mosaic technique of the Roman past, or else had revived devices of that past. Selective revivals and survivals of this kind were frequent, and it is not always possible to differentiate clearly between the two. Both are among the phenomena which add to the complexity of the process of stylistic evolution.

A work such as the Beth-Alpha floor, on the other hand, virtually stands outside that evolution and is remarkable for that very reason. Here are two folk artists speaking their own minds, as it were, unfettered by traditions and conventions, and thus establishing a fresh and direct rapport with the beholder. They do not, for instance, feel bound by the rule fundamental to all ancient art since the classical age of Greece, that there should be balance in the proportioning of the parts of a body, and an even, eurhythmic flow in fusing these parts into a whole. By their standards even the relatively abstract leopard of Caesarea (Plate 26) is still classical. Their own quadrupeds are amorphous shapes to which are attached with startling abruptness and no consistency of scale the several features typical of the species concerned (Plate 13). The lack of balance and of rhythmic responses is as characteristic of groups of figures as it is of the component parts of single figures. It is interesting, for instance, to compare the men leading the donkey in the scene of the Sacrifice of Isaac with a similar motif at Beth-Shean which may be of nearly the same date (Plates 10 and 18). In neither instance were man and beast drawn to a consistent scale. But at Beth-Shean their contours and movements are at least interrelated and complementary, while the leading servant at Beth-Alpha is compositionally quite disjointed from the animal (to say nothing of the figure's intrinsic lack of proportion, cohesion, and consistency) and connected with it only in the most literal sense, namely, through the rein he holds in his hands.

The design of faces shows the same independence from the established traditions of the craft. The artists have their own stereotyped formula for this. No matter how intricate the movement of figures, heads are always *en face*, there is a strong emphasis on the eyes as the most telling and expressive feature, and six white strokes, tenuously and incongruously appended to an otherwise youthful countenance, serve to characterize Abraham as the ageing patriarch (Plates 8 and 9). The use of colour is also unconventional. Coloured tesserae are applied in solid surfaces without any attempt at shading or modelling. As

20

Khirbet el-Minya, Ummaiyyad Palace. General view of geometric pavement (see detail, Plate 28). Eighth century. Photo: Deutscher Verein vom Heiligen Lande.

a result there is barely any suggestion of a third dimension, the less so since sizeable portions of many figures are rendered in the same neutral grey-white as the background. Colour was used primarily for the sake of expression and emphasis. It picks out faces, hands, significant parts of costume, and essential attributes and paraphernalia. In the case of the Sacrifice of Isaac it picks out the fateful knife and the wildly contorted right arm which holds it, but not the left (Plate 8).

Thus the intent of the mosaicists becomes clear. Their primary concerns were literalness and clarity. Theirs is, in a sense, a timeless art. They are indebted to the conventions of the period mainly for their themes, for the ornamental framework, and for descriptive detail such as costumes. Their renderings are largely their own and bear every indication of being a direct and personal response to the subjects at hand.

Let us return once more to the main stream of the development, which so far we have considered only in terms of single figures or groups. We have seen how three-dimensional bodies were blended increasingly into surface patterns (for the Beth-Alpha artists, incidentally, this was no problem; their figures were *a priori* part of the surface). This acceptance of the surface as a basis of the design, however, involves not only individual figures; it became during the period which concerns us here a key factor in the layout and composition of the floor as a whole.

To appreciate this development fully we must look back for a moment to the Roman period. The centuries from the first to the third were the great era of *trompe-l'œil* effects. We need only think of Pompeian wall-paintings with their simulated architectures and their vistas of imaginary gardens and landscapes, which lead the eye into the distance and make us forget that we are actually confined within solid walls. Such devices were applied to floor decoration also. The floor, too, or at least some section thereof, was made to appear—most incongruously —as though it were open space. Often its principal feature was a panel, or a series of panels, affording what appear to be glimpses into the distance in which figures or groups of figures move freely. These picture panels—the so-called emblemata—were like so many windows seemingly perforating the surface and dissembling its uniform solidity. In the countries of the Eastern Mediterranean this type of floor decoration, which teases the beholder by denying the solidity of the ground he steps on, had found particular favour and was often executed with great ingenuity and skill. Beginning with the fourth century, however, artists increasingly reacted against this concept of the floor. Instead of breaking into the surface and opening up distant views, they more and more accepted that surface in its entirety and in its solidity as a basis of their compositions. The " window " gives way to the " carpet ".

Of the pavements in Israel here illustrated, only the hunting frieze of Beth-Guvrin still has a clear suggestion of an open scenery (Plates 4 and 5). In all other instances the artist has used compositional devices based on the principle of the acceptance of the surface. The most interesting of these devices is the one employed in the Nilotic scenes at Tabgha. The artist has taken the landscape to pieces and has scattered its component parts over the surface. The device as such is traditional. It has remote antecedents in Hellenistic and Roman mosaics simulating unswept floors, a typical *jeu d'esprit* of that period whereby left-overs from a banquet, rendered so realistically that they might be taken for the real thing, were shown strewn over the surface as though they had just been dropped by a host of diners. To adapt this principle of composition to a landscape, as was done at Tabgha, was an extraordinary idea. The aim here was not to create illusion, but, on the contrary, to destroy it. Since there is no staging in depth, no impression of distance can arise. All objects are on a single plane, the plane of the floor itself, which asserts itself openly and as a unified surface. This anti-illusionism is fundamental to the composition of the Tabgha landscapes, even though, as we have seen, individual figures still retain a three-dimensional appearance, and the backgrounds, as a result, a certain ambiguity.

The simplest way of proclaiming the unity and solidity of the floor surface was to cover it evenly and uniformly with a single geometric pattern, or a series of patterns. Floors with this type of design enjoyed a great vogue in the late fourth century. No doubt the puritanism which the Church displayed at that period—a movement already mentioned above—reinforced the trend. But the unified carpet design also satisfied an aesthetic bent, and increasingly from this time on figure subjects were made a part of such designs (Plates 19 to 21, 27). A further characteristic development occurred in the sixth century when a vine *rinceau* often took the place of a geometric framework for the figures to be fitted into. The stems of the vine are so flat and their convolutions so regular that the effect is still that of an abstract pattern, albeit in a superficially organic disguise (Plates 17 and 18, 22 to 24).

None of these compositional devices was entirely new. They all have Roman antecedents (some of them more especially in the West). But they here come into their own as so many ways of asserting the material existence of the floor surface, and of making the decoration co-extensive with that surface. Our earlier observations on the style of single figures must be considered in the light of this evolving concept of the floor as a whole. Most of those figures and groups that blend so well into their backgrounds and make such satisfying ensembles with their frames are, in fact, parts of unified carpet designs (Plates 17 to 24, 27). The marvel is that in becoming parts of all-over patterns they yet retain so strong an air of reality. The reconciliation of abstract pattern and organic life was a major objective in all Byzantine art. In the floor mosaics of the early Byzantine period it was realized within the confines of a traditional craft, and nowhere more successfully than in Palestine.

ILLUSTRATIONS

8

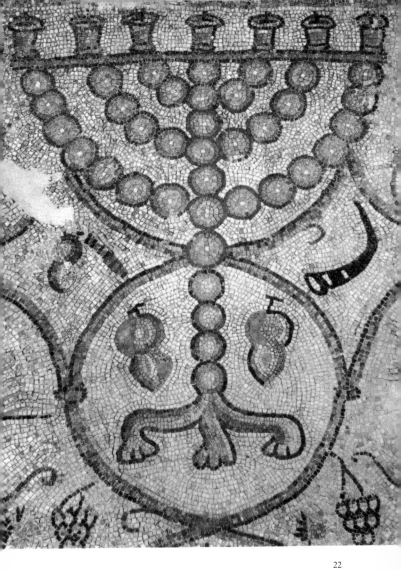

26

BIBLIOGRAPHY

Some works on floor mosaics in other areas in the Near East are also included in this bibliography.

Actes du premier colloque international sur la mosaïque (Paris, 29 août - 3 septembre 1963), Paris, 1965 (in the press).

AVI-YONAH, Michael, *Mosaic pavements in Palestine*, London, Oxford University Press, 1934 (reprinted from: *Quarterly of the Department of Antiquities in Palestine*, II & III).

AVI-YONAH, Michael, The ancient synagogue of Maʿon (Nirim): the mosaic pavement, *Bulletin of the Louis M. Rabinowitz Fund for the Exploration of Ancient Synagogues*, vol. III, 1960, pp. 25-35.

FITZGERALD, Gerald. M., *A sixth-century monastery at Beth-Shan*, Philadelphia, University of Pennsylvania Press, 1939 (Publications of the Palestine Section of the University Museum, University of Pennsylvania, IV).

GOODENOUGH, Erwin R., *Jewish symbols in the Greco-Roman period*, especially vols. I & III, New York, Pantheon Books, 1953 (Bollingen series, 37).

GRABAR, André, Recherches sur les sources juives de l'art paléochrétien, *Cahiers archéologiques*, vol. XI, 1960, pp. 41-71; vol. XII, 1962, pp. 115-52.

Israel—Ancient mosaics, preface by Meyer Schapiro, introduction by Michael Avi-Yonah, New York, New York Graphic Society (by arrangement with Unesco), 1960 (Unesco world art series).

KITZINGER, Ernst, *Mosaic pavements in the Greek East and the question of a "Renaissance" under Justinian, Actes du VIe Congrès international d'études byzantines*, Paris, 1948, vol. II, pp. 209-23, Paris, École des hautes études, 1951.

LAVIN, Irving, The hunting mosaics of Antioch and their sources: a study of compositional principles in the development of early mediaeval style, *Dumbarton Oaks papers*, vol. 17, 1963, pp. 179-286.

LEVI, Doro, *Antioch mosaic pavements*, Princeton, Princeton University Press, 1947, 2 vols. (Publications of the Committee for the Excavation of Antioch and its Vicinity, 4).

MOREY, Charles R., *The mosaics of Antioch*, London - New York - Toronto, Longmans, Green, 1938.

SCHNEIDER, Alfons M., *The Church of the Multiplying of the Loaves and Fishes at Tabgha on the Lake of Gennesaret and its mosaics*, ed. A.A. Gordon, London, Alexander Ouseley, 1937.

STERN, Henri, *Pavements d'Israël: exposition de reproductions en couleurs*, Paris, 1963.

SUKENIK, Eleazar L., *The ancient synagogue of Beth Alpha*, Jerusalem, University Press; London, Oxford University Press, 1932.

TRENDALL, Arthur D., *The Shellal mosaic*, 2nd ed., Canberra, Australian War Memorial, 1957.

CONTENTS

The colour photography for the illustrations in this book was carried out by a special Unesco mission which visited Israel for this purpose and to collect the necessary documentation. This mission worked in close conjunction with the governmental authorities of Israel, and Unesco wishes to express its appreciation to all those who collaborated in this work.

Introduction by Ernst Kitzinger . . . . . Page 5

Heptapegon (et Tabgha), Church of the Multiplication of Loaves and Fishes. Pavement in north wing of transept: water birds, lotus and other water plants. Fifth century . . . Plate 1

Heptapegon (et Tabgha), Church of the Multiplication of Loaves and Fishes. Pavement in north wing of transept: bird and city wall. Fifth century . . . . . Plate 2

Heptapegon (et Tabgha), Church of the Multiplication of Loaves and Fishes. Pavement behind altar: basket with loaves, two fishes. Fifth century . . . . Plate 3

Beth-Guvrin, villa. Border of pavement: huntsman. Fifth century . . . . Plate 4

Beth-Guvrin, villa. Border of pavement: running hare. Fifth century . . . . . . Plate 5

Shavey Zion, church. Pavement: cross in medallion. Fifth century . . . . . . Plate 6

Shavey Zion, church. Geometric pavement (detail). Fifth century . . . . . . Plate 7

Beth-Alpha, synagogue, pavement. The Sacrifice of Isaac: Abraham and Isaac. Sixth century . . . Plate 8

Beth-Alpha, synagogue, pavement. The Sacrifice of Isaac: Abraham. Sixth century . . . . Plate 9

Beth-Alpha, synagogue, pavement. The Sacrifice of Isaac: servants leading donkey. Sixth century . . . Plate 10

Beth-Alpha, synagogue, pavement. Zodiac Panel: heads of horses from the Chariot of the Sun. Sixth century . Plate 11

Beth-Alpha, synagogue, pavement. Zodiac Panel: sign of the Virgin. Sixth century . . . . Plate 12

Beth-Alpha, synagogue. Border of pavement: bull flanking inscription at entrance. Sixth century . . . Plate 13

Beth-Alpha, synagogue. Border of pavement: hen with chicks. Sixth century . . . . . Plate 14

Beth-Shean, monastery of the Lady Mary. Pavement with the personifications of the Months: head of February. Probably 569 after Christ . . . . . Plate 15

Beth-Shean, monastery of the Lady Mary. Pavement with the personifications of the Months: head of October. Probably 569 after Christ . . . . . Plate 16

Beth-Shean, monastery of the Lady Mary. Vine trellis pavement: man playing flute to his dog. Probably 569 after Christ . . . . . . Plate 17

Beth-Shean, monastery of the Lady Mary. Vine trellis pavement: negro leading animal. Probably 569 after Christ . . . . Plate 18

Tiberias, bath. Pavement: beribboned bird. Sixth century Plate 19

Tiberias, bath. Pavement: crane. Sixth century . . Plate 20

Tiberias, bath. Pavement: duck. Sixth century . . Plate 21

Nirim, synagogue of Maʿon. Pavement: seven-branched candelabrum. Sixth century . . . . Plate 22

Nirim, synagogue of Maʿon. Pavement: leopard. Sixth century . . . . Plate 23

Nirim, synagogue of Maʿon. Pavement: hen and egg. Sixth century . . . . Plate 24

Huldah. Pavement: seven-branched candelabrum, ritual utensils and Greek inscription "Blessing to the People". Sixth century . . . . . . Plate 25

Caesarea, church outside the walls. Border of pavement: leopard. Late sixth century . . . . Plate 26

Caesarea, church outside the walls. Pavement: pelican. Late sixth century . . . . . Plate 27

Khirbet el-Minya, Ummaiyyad palace. Geometric pavement (detail). Eighth century . . . . Plate 28

Printed in Italy